How To Get Your Child Into
the College of Your Their Dreams
- without cheating
bonus story "Peaks"

Chapter 1 - The Why

My first disclaimer is this book is based on an eleven year process. If your student, who we will call child throughout this book, will change their college major more than, I would say underwear but we know children do not always change their underwear, their mind then this instruction manual may not work .

One of the most powerful driving factors in college application success is in having a "story". My student, daughter, developed a magnificent story built through trials, tribulations, and triumphs. In some circles this is known as your "why". It is the reason why she has maintained incredible focus for the past 12 years and is now attending the college of my, I mean her, dreams . I would strongly suggest that you delve into the "why" answer a little more by also purchasing a book by Simon Sinek titled, "Start With Why" .

In 2007, our family of three, plus Anna our German Shorthaired Pointer, lived in Gypsum, Colorado . During this time I was working a forty hour a week day job, and hotel night audit (third shift) on the weekend. My fitness and training goals, at that time, were built around training for a 70.3 half Ironman triathlon.

The events of June 10, 2007, are all based on hearsay as I do not remember the events of that day as well as two or three weeks after . From midnight of that day, until eight in the morning, I worked the audit shift at the Evergreen Lodge in Vail, Colorado . Between ten in the morning and noon we attended New Creation Church of Glenwood Springs as a family. We had lunch and then I took a short nap. I woke up during late afternoon, got ready, and set out on my Trek 1000 road bicycle intent on riding Glenwood Canyon both ways .

Just west of Gypsum the bike trail descends and there is a switchback around a gully. I had set up my Trek with triathlon aerobars on which you semi-lay when you ride. In recreating what must have happened I was probably half asleep when I approached the bend in the trail, was possibly traveling about fifty miles per hour, I had a bad habit of raising with my right hand which controls the front brake, flipped my bike, landed on my head, and broke my helmet into several pieces .

My wife tells me she received a phone call that evening from the Eagle County Paramedic Service stating they found me on a trail, I was unresponsive, and they could not find a pulse . She told them my pulse was low as I worked out a lot. Even today, many years later, my resting pulse is in the high forties or low fifties. They checked again and found my heart-rate was in the thirties. The EMT's were led to me by a lady whose dog found me while they were out for a walk. Thank you dog with the lady with the phone!

Lifeflight took me to St. Mary's Hospital in Grand Junction, Colorado where I was diagnosed with a Traumatic Brain Injury or TBI . After a short time, a couple of weeks there I think , my wife had me transferred to Valley View Hospital in Glenwood Springs . From there I ended up at Craig Hospital in Englewood which is a Denver suburb.

Our daughter was eleven years old during these happenings and spent a lot of time with me at the hospital as it was summer and my wife had to work in Edwards . Because she spent so much time with me the therapist at St. Mary's and Valley View recruited her to help with homework therapy in the evenings . For Speech Therapy she would make me work with flash cards showing pictures of objects I had to identify . The Physical Therapist would have her work on balancing skills with me which she took way too much delight in .

However , it was Occupational Therapy which she fell in love with. I won't go into the rest of the recovery here as this book is about college applications and not a single TBI recovery.

During the summer of 2008 my wife and I began to discuss moving back to Central Kansas to help her mother with her home and large garden . In addition we discussed the differences in education between Colorado and Kansas. In the end we chose to move back to Reno County where we were originally from as on a national scale Kansas education was held in higher esteem than Colorado .

Chapter 2 - Pick Your Major

As alluded to in the "foreword" Renee' developed a story at age eleven. I am aware most children are not as fortunate in that regard, and I certainly hope a similar accident is not in your future. There are ways though to develop a "story" or "why" in your student. Get them involved with a local church, your church, or any type of place of worship. Have them travel on mission or outreach trips. Make sure they volunteer locally for any and every type of need. Encourage your student to work odd jobs and experience your local community. If you can, send them on an international trip or several. They will find their passion in doing these things. The goal here is to not keep them in a bubble of yours, or their, making. Our goal always was for Renee' to know the world was much bigger, and had a lot more to offer, than just Central Kansas.

In working to help them develop their "why" the journey may take them down many paths; as mine did. Work with your student to develop a focus and narrow it down to one or two major "things". The plan is to prevent a frequent change in Major's as what happened to me in college. You know the pun about underwear? This is why I am not a medical doctor. I changed Major's too often.

Again, a great place to research the best, as well as the most prominent, up and coming careers is through https://money.usnews.com/careers/best-jobs/rankings . Be creative. Do not just match your child's interest with a job title. Look deeper within the job and find hidden and deeper activities and focus that interest your child. The enemy of the best career is boredom.

Choosing the right Major, not only for the prerequisite Bachelor's Degree program, but also the Master's and Doctoral level is important not only to your student's future and livelihood, but also the pocketbook and finances of everyone involved.

So what is your students' story? Do they have one yet? My suggestion would be to get one! In the meantime Renee' presented us with what she wanted to do. In order to validate her idea, and make sure it was a viable profession, we started researching the outlook of the Occupational Therapy profession and we started with https://money.usnews.com/careers/best-jobs and https://collegegrad.com/careers . Thankfully, she had chosen a field that was expected to grow exponentially over the next decade or two which would solidify her future. I pray your students story, or desire, does not lead them down an obscure path. If so, I hope for a great foundational network to help them succeed.

Because we were aiming for grad school all along Renee' needed to start with a focused bachelor's degree. It was similar to being a "prerequisite". We visited many websites for Occupational Therapy to research popular major's for her future field. There may be many for your field as well. Target one that brings the most "bang for your buck" to the party. Pardon the puns. She went with an extremely versatile field which will hopefully open doors worldwide into the future.

Renee' started with a Sociology undergraduate degree which will enable her to adapt to various cultures and habitats worldwide. "It is the study of the development, structure, and functioning of human society."(a) How we do things in Haven, Kansas is different than inner city Los Angeles or even Chicago. This first degree will help her pair it with Occupational Therapy so she can most fully treat patients while still respecting their culture. When you do not tread on sociological toes the treatments tend to be more successful. You need to keep nuances such as this in mind as you choose a four year degree and then grad school. (a) google Dictionary

Chapter 3 - Pick the Right High School

My wife and I researched and discussed the differences in high schools between Gypsum, Colorado and the area in Kansas which we were planning to return to. The return to help with a family member was priority one in going back to where we grew up in Kansas. Priority two was to give our daughter a chance at the best education possible.

One of the first places we looked for high school, and later college, information was with the U.S. News and World Report at   https://www.usnews.com/education/best-high-schools . U.S. News and World Report at https://www.usnews.com/education/ has an extensive database of school and university information which is invaluable in research and in choosing schools. However, in addition to national rankings we also used our personal knowledge of the local schools. There were several which we knew from experience would have set her back years in information, knowledge, and future opportunities. I went to a high school where my graduating class was over three hundred in size. This effectively helped me disappear among the overachievers. I placed in the top twenty percent in terms of class grade scoring, but otherwise was lost among the numbers. My wife attended a very small school where one could be homecoming queen or king, score in the top one percent, be the valedictorian, hold the class president title, and various other exemplary resume entries based on a class size of five.

When we moved back to Kansas, in August of 2008, Renee' was entering seventh grade so we enrolled her in the local grade school in our town of around 300. This elementary school, three blocks from our new home, taught grades from kindergarten through eighth grade, and served many small towns in this part of the county. There was a great teacher to student ratio, of about 20:1, and the principal was one of my wife's teachers when she was in grade school. The school was part of a local school system which received good grades in education according to U.S. News and World Report.

While in Colorado, Renee was introduced to algebra, but an introduction was as far as it went. During my research on education I found many girls were not excelling in, or being educated in, the sciences or mathematics at that time (now part of STEM). I made a determination Renee' was going to be an exception to the rule. As she was ready to enter eighth grade we decided she should take pre-algebra. The principal did not want to let her in based partly on a bias toward my wife and partly because she was a girl. I had a stern meeting in his office where he washed his hands of the outcome and let her enroll. Other than holding the high score in class, taking college algebra in high school, and college trigonometry at the community college, while holding "A" grades in all of them, the results were pretty much what we expected. This helped lay a foundation for later classes in her Doctoral program.

August of 2010, was when she started high school. Her school was about twenty miles from where we lived so she started her high school career the way she had finished it in Colorado; by taking the bus. Not only did she excel in mathematics, but she also took an introductory Anatomy and Physiology class which would pay huge dividends later. The beauty (part of) was her high school teamed up with the local community college to offer classes with college credits while still in high school.

Renee's high school career was full of many highlights and we will go into those in the next chapter. She graduated in 2014, and was ranked in the top five percent of her class. Because of how well she did she was offered many scholarships; one of which paid for ninety-percent of her first three years of college.

At the end of May, and first of June, 2014 I took her to Sydney, Australia for her graduation present and to attend the International Rotary Convention. The convention featured speakers who represent my daughter's future clientele, and helped fuel her fire toward uni.

Chapter 4 - Resume' or Curriculum Vitae, Clubs, Community Service, and Find Other Opportunities

In college application, as much or more than in business, a resume', or Curriculum Vitae is vital in preparation and college acceptance. A resume' is a concise document which simply gives an overview of what your child has done in their school and social career. This chapter mentions the resume', but I would strongly suggest that you focus instead on a CV, or Curriculum Vitae which usually goes into much more detail than a resume'.

Columbia University states at https://www.careereducation.columbia.edu/resources/what-curriculum-vitae , a CV "is a detailed and comprehensive description of your academic credentials and achievements. You will use a CV if you're a master's degree-holder or PhD applying for a teaching or research position at a college, university, or research institution. You may also use your CV during graduate school to apply for grants, fellowships, or teaching positions." Hence my suggestion is to use it for all college applications.

A first question might be, "at what age should we start building a CV?" My answer would be "as soon as possible." We began building Renee's even before we began speaking, or even thinking about, college. When she was three she began figure skating. This built a winning attitude and someone who can dream big dreams. She also became a team player through her skating years by watching and willing her teammates to win. When we moved to Colorado we withdrew her from skating as there were almost no coaches in the mountains we felt comfortable with. In elementary school, because she did not now have skating to fuel her competitiveness, Renee' began to try volleyball as a sport. Also, at age ten we enrolled her in 4H in Eagle County, Colorado. 4H helped with her social skills and other things such as sewing, the shooting sports, she earned a babysitting proficiency certificate, and began to develop business acumen. She began to learn how to play the flute, but most elementary school concerts at this stage were hair pulling and fingernails on chalkboards affairs which were suffered through at great lengths. Again, while in Colorado she began to build her "why" because of my accident and we subsequently moved back to Central Kansas. Her curriculum vitae did not grow a lot while in middle school, but took off like a rocket during her high school years! In middle school, beside the aforementioned enrollment in algebra, she stepped up her musical skills and studied under the wife of her future high school music teacher. This husband and wife team were the best in the county. She taught students the great foundational basics, and her husband later built upon those. These concerts finally helped our family graduate past the hair pulling and were actually enjoyable. The music training helped to develop the non-STEM parts of her brain like empathy.

Renee's Freshman year in high school laid the foundation for a lot of her later development. She ran for "public" office and became the Freshman class president. This became habitual and she held the Sophomore, Junior, and Student Body presidency's, as a Senior, as well. Her later candidacy's, and run's for office, were helped by the four years she spent in forensics.

Forensics is similar to sports in that it is a competitive event entered into by those in high school. It centers around public speaking and uses a prepared version as well as the extemporaneous form. The prepared presentation is usually one which is memorized and given at each Forensics Tournament throughout the year. The extemporaneous speech begins with a topic which is chosen at the tournament, includes a thirty minute preparation period, and which is then given as a completely prepared discourse. Not only did she place very high in state competitions, but Renee' eventually gave a keynote address at her junior college's graduation in front of over two-thousand people! I would suggest forensics, or even debate, for the reasons of building a confidence in speaking in front of groups of people. However, this ability can also translate into effective speaking for college interviews up to and including for bachelor's, master's, and doctoral level entry. It certainly worked in Renee's case.

She decided, when she entered high school, she was not good enough in sports to compete at the level required to shine on a consistent basis. This is one reason she chose forensics, but Renee' also continued her playing of the flute, added piccolo, and was involved with her marching and pep bands through all four years. The music teacher from the local high school was one of the, if not the, best in the state. Her final award was a Patrick S Gilmore for outstanding contribution. The four years she spent with the members of the band helped shape her excellent social skills as well as giving her a team mentality. There are many ways for your student to develop the same skills. If there are siblings in the mix then you will have differing dynamics. In a different chapter I will cover competencies which will be important in your future college acceptance.

As I spoke about earlier, during her junior year, Renee' took an introductory course in anatomy and physiology (A&P) which played a large role in her college success. Our local community college is well known for its' nursing program However, it has not always known such reknown. During its' early years many prospective nurses washed out of the program after taking the extremely difficult A&P class. The college remade the program, created an extremely difficult one semester A&P curriculum, and required it to be taken within the first two semesters of starting college. Because of this, students would know in the early stages whether they were going to stay in the nursing program or whether they needed to make a change in major. Not only did Renee' pass the class with an A+; she also later tutored other students who washed out on their first attempt.

A lot of these resume' items, pre high school, were accidental or not planned for the college application process. However, once she entered high school the whole paradigm changed. When it all boiled down we spent the next eight years planning every single move. So much so this book is born partially on all of the free time I now have!

As alluded to earlier, even choosing the geographical area, as well as the actual high school, were done deliberately to give Renee' the best chance to fully succeed. My intent is not to give anyone a guilt trip, but much of her success was due to my wife and I's heavy involvement in her life, school path, and social interactions. We took nothing for granted in our attempt to build a well-rounded young lady.

We spoke of this earlier, but Renee' ran for class president during her first year of high school. Because I had campaigned to be elected state representative, though I did not win, the skills were developed for a campaign which she adapted to her successful run for office. I wish I had used some of her campaign ideas. She also enrolled in Spanish, was a flautist for the pep band, played the same instrument for marching band, and was a member of the "Trash Cats" which was a percussion group which banged on anything that created a percussive melody.

Renee' enrolled in local community college classes, while in high school, and knocked out college algebra, college trigonometry, and writing composition to name three.

Her yearly campaigns for class president were also helped by her freshman year enrollment in forensics. She has never been shy, but forensics helped her develop extreme confidence in public speaking. As mentioned earlier, so much so she spoke eloquently to over two-thousand people at her junior college graduation.

Also, somewhere in the middle of these four years we developed, as a family, a penchant for volunteerism. My wife and I volunteered, and still do, for many local causes. This set up a great model for Renee' to follow and follow it she did.

For the first three years she was successful in her attempts to be elected class president, and for her senior year she became to student body president. During her fourth year she also qualified for the state tournament in forensics. In her tenure at this school she may have earned one B+ grade, but the rest were certainly all A's. Trust me; for the B+ there were tears. In her whole academic career she does not simply dislike B's and lower. She despises them.

While she was a senior I re-immersed myself in Rotary International, and also found a service group called AMBUCS. The AMBUCS mission is to provide mobility for those with disabilities as well as to fund scholarships for physical, speech, or occupational therapy students. The scholarships were what caught my attention. Our local AMBUCS's biggest fundraiser, to the tune of mid-five figures, was to operate a waffle cone and ice cream building every September at the Kansas State Fair. Renee' spent many hours as a volunteer, as did I, as well as being the special speaker on several occasions at our clubs meetings.

During attendance, at our local junior college, Renee' was the recipient of a Presidential Leadership Scholarship. One of the qualifying marks for this was to have forty or more hours of community service over two years of junior college. At the large scholarship festival, where she again spoke to the attendees, it was mentioned Renee' had more than four hundred hours of volunteer work to her credit during the aforementioned two years.

At the local level, in addition to being the junior college student body president, she was also a Phi Theta Kappa officer, the chair of a few drives for blood and other projects, a social dance club member, the co-founder of a couple of clubs, part of leadership for Circle K International, and a junior Rotarian. One of the clubs she helped start later became a local church, which ministers to the underserved population in our local county seat, which has become the foundation for her doctoral capstone. As alluded to earlier she was a tutor for A&P, and was active in Vacation Bible School locally every summer. This started at our church, but eventually Renee' was leading VBS all over town. This finally culminated in her joining a VBS on the road troupe one summer and ended up in south Texas. She was not only able to work with many Hispanic children with disabilities, but it also helped finish her education of the Spanish language which she had taken in school for two years in high school and two semesters in junior college. She often commented Vacation Bible School was her version of vacation and she still leads it wherever in the world she can find one.

While in Edinburgh Renee' joined a woman's choir which sang during Christmas. She was also active in many local clubs, causes, and places of worship.

When she came back to the states, and attended the University of Kansas, she was again immersed in Circle K, but she also started her own club named "Recipe 4 Life" which was under the umbrella of the Christian Union and Intervarsity.

A very important addition to your students CV will be clubs. If you would like to research top clubs for college application consideration go to https://www.usnews.com/best-colleges/rankings . For

Renee' she was a part of AMBUCS, Rotary International, Circle K International, Social Dance Club, Intervarsity, Spark (which she co-founded), Christian Union (the parent of Intervarsity), Recipe 4 Life (which she also founded), and (vocal choir).

In 2013 I worked as a sales manager for a water and fire restoration company. As the sales manager I was immersed in the local chamber of commerce and convention and visitors bureau events and attended a "State of the City" presentation that was sponsored by the local AMBUCS chapter. AMBUCS stands for American Business Clubs, was founded in 1922, and they provide mobility for people with disabilities. They also fund scholarships for therapists who will help with the same patients with disabilities. They gave a short program to show what they stand for and everything aligned with my daughter's plans. I gave my intent to join prior to leaving this meeting. Over time Renee' and I gave countless hours to the group and it culminated with my Presidency of the local club. In addition, she gave presentations at our Friday meetings about the Circle K Leadership camp, her trip to Spain, her trip to Italy and France, our trip to Australia for the Rotary International Convention in Sydney in 2014, and finally her year at uni in Edinburgh. The local chapter has been extremely supportive of her and she was awarded several scholarships by the local group as well as her latest national award from the national office. Their link can be found at   https://ambucs.org.

This is Renee's CV:

Renee' M. R.

EDUCATION

OTD Studies-Sargent College-Boston University
   September 2018-May 2021

· Accepted into the Doctoral Occupational Therapy program for the fall of 2018

· Anticipated graduation date is spring of 2021

BA Studies-Sociology-University of Kansas   August 2017-May 2018

· Undergraduate Research: analysis of the ADA Resource Center for Equity and Accessibility Policy at the University of Kansas

· Graduated with a Bachelor of Arts in Sociology

BA Studies-Sociology-University of Edinburgh September 2016-May 2017

· Studied Sociology, Psychology, and Cultural Anthropology in preparation for Occupational Therapy studies

BA Studies-Sociology-Wichita State University   August 2014-May 2016

· Studied Sociology courses while attending Hutchinson Community College

AA Studies-Hutchinson Community College   August 2014-May 2016

· Studied Sociology and pre-Occupational Therapy

· Graduated with an Associate of Arts degree

EXPERIENCE

Blessed Mess Baked Goods

May 2018-Present

Owner

· Began a donation-based baking business as a pathway to fund my higher education.

· Take orders, bake, and deliver the baked goods to customers.

· Collaborated with a local coffee shop to sell baked goods.

Journey Mennonite Youth Intern, South Hutchinson, KS **May-August 2017**

Journey Youth Intern
· Filled all duties of the youth pastor, as he was on sabbatical (created and organized middle school and high school curriculum, preached on Sunday evenings, planned games and summer outings for the students - including weekly activities for the middle school girls, attended weekly prayer and pastoral meetings, among other secretarial duties)
· Met with the lead pastor once a week, and read books (such as *The Forgotten Ways Handbook*) , to dedicate time to my personal development

Traveling Vacation Bible School, Hesston, KS
May-August 2016
Director
· Helped with curriculum, acting, and leadership with traveling Vacation Bible School team to south Texas and Kansas City.
· Worked one-on-one and as a group leader of children with differing special needs.

Hutchinson Community College Tutor, Hutchinson, KS
January-May 2016
Tutor
· Met one-on-one with tutees for one hour sessions 2-3 times a week.
· Tutored in Anatomy and Physiology, General Biology, and Abnormal Psychology.
· Evaluated tutees learning style and created a learning atmosphere that promoted their strengths to enhance their weaknesses.

Babysitter/Nanny, Hutchinson and Marion, KS
May 2009-Current
Caretaker
· Cared for 1-16 children from 6 months-12 years old.

· Tasks include feeding, changing diapers, potty training, encouraging responsibility (cleaning up toys, caring for pets), alternative discipline methods, morning and bedtime routines (showers, brushing teeth, making beds), and increasing life experience (baking, science experiments, museums, etc.).

· Care ranged from 4 hours-24 hours a day.

In-Home Care for COPD Patient Hutchinson, KS
August 2011-December 2011
Caretaker

· Cared for an elderly lady diagnosed with COPD.

· Tasks ranged from cooking, cleaning, and doing laundry, to reading, shopping, and running errands.

· Care ranged from 10-14 hours, usually in the afternoons and through the night.

ACTIVITIES AND LEADERSHIP

- Student Government Public Relations Officer (SGA)
- Student Body President at Hutchinson Community College (HCC), 2015-2016
- Helped lead Kick Butt's Day - tobacco prevention and awareness
- Ran American Red Cross Blood Drive with record breaking numbers
- Was a team leader for the Reno County American Heart Association
- SGA canned food drive: raised 54 pounds of food
- SGA Toys for Tots: collected 55 toys (the record for HCC).
- SGA American Red Cross Blood Drive: record amount of blood given at HCC

- I was on the committee for the Red Flag Campaign (dating violence awareness program) for HCC
- Represented the Student Body on the Dillon Lecture Series Committee, and the Teaching and Learning Committee for HCC.
- Represented the HCC Student Body for the Higher Learning Commission (HLC) during the accreditation period.
- Attended the American Student Government Association Conference in Washington, D.C.
- Member of Circle K International (CKI)
- Trunk or Treat for Unicef
- Set up for the TECH, Inc (Training and Evaluation Center of Hutchinson) Christmas Gala for individuals with disabilities
- Attended a city clean up day in Emporia, KS
- Attended Circle K District Convention in Manhattan, KS
- Attended Circle K International Convention in Toronto, Canada
- Led a service project in Toronto, Canada with the members of Aktion Club (individuals with disabilities)
- Recognized at the CKI Kansas District Service Member of the Year with over 600 service hours for the 2015-2016 school year
- Leadership Academy (Circle K) Graduate 2015
- Member of Phi Theta Kappa (PTK)
- Phi Theta Kappa Officer
- Volunteered at the St. Jude's Children's Research Hospital Marathon, December 2015

- Recognized as a Distinguished PTK Officer for the 2015-2016 school year
- Attended Phi Theta Kappa Nerd Nation International Convention in Washington, D.C.
- PTK Officers organized No-Shave November to raise money for Cancer Council of Reno County.
- PTK Officers organized Coat Drive: coats donated to the people in the community that needed them most.
- Vice President of HCC SPARK (Students Planting a Revival for the Kingdom); affiliated with InterVarsity
- A chartering member of SPARK
- Attended Catalyst - InterVarsity (SPARK) Camp
- Member of Social Dance Club at HCC
- Social Dance Club Chair
- 900+ hours of community service to date during my university career
- Taught 4th and 5th graders on Sunday mornings at Journey Mennonite Church (3 years)
- Led worship for Children's Church on Sunday mornings at Journey Mennonite Church (3 years)
- Led Vacation Bible School (VBS) for 4 churches in 2015
- Led VBS for 10 years at Journey Mennonite Church of South Hutchinson
- Taught Bible lessons to less fortunate 5th and 6th graders on Wednesday evenings (1 year)
- Traveled to Spain, France and Italy (donated clothes for the homeless in the Vatican City and Madrid)
- Junior Rotarian for Rotary International

- Attended the International Rotarian Convention in Sydney, Australia in 2014
- Served ice cream at the Kansas State Fair for the AMBUCS fundraiser, 2014-2016
- Studied abroad in Edinburgh, Scotland for the 2016-2017 school year (200+ service hours)
- On the welcome team at the Christian Union (CU)
- Cooked meals and served the student community during Something More Events Week (CU).
- Participated in CU Text-A-Toasty (answering questions about God door to door).
- Volunteered at Lunch Bars (CU) to hand out free tea and coffee and to serve lunch and clean up.
- Organized an Operation Christmas Child (Samaritan's Purse) event where we were able to fill 15 shoeboxes that were sent to Romania for Christmas, 2017
- Organized an international Thanksgiving meal for my accommodation in Edinburgh.
- Helped raise over £200 for the Edinburgh Women's Rape and Sexual Abuse Centre with the Female Voice Choir.
- C3 Edinburgh Kids Church leader
- C3 Edinburgh Praise team member
- CPR training
- Attended the 2017 Global Leadership Summit as the youth intern at Journey Mennonite Church in Hutchinson, KS
- Started a baking ministry on campus at the University of Kansas, The Recipe for Life, for international students

- Team member of International Friends (through InterVarsity) at the University of Kansas
- Attended the multicultural conference, Corners Conference 2018, in Overland Park, KS
- Graduate Student Intern at Hale House (Assisted living facility) for 8 weeks, fall 2018
- Led a national backpack awareness initiative at a Boston public school, fall 2018
- Volunteered with Boston University Rotaract for backpack awareness at Brookline Town Day, fall 2018
- Raised money for, and packed, 6 shoeboxes for Operation Christmas Child (Samaritan's Purse) with international students for Christmas, 2018
- Organized and hosted a baking fundraiser for the American Occupational Therapy Association conference, 2018

Chapter 5 - Instill Humility

Interestingly enough this was fairly easy to do with Renee'. She was raised as lower-middle class as I had the accident and then did not make great career decisions for several years (okay, a decade) after. The only reason she even knew what a silver spoon was was because I inherited a silver utensil set from my grandmother, and we certainly did not let her put them in her mouth.

She learned to be grateful for what we did provide and gifts we periodically received. Her first car was given to her after she and my wife cleaned a cat ladies home. Boy did the car smell great. Renee' did not get to run around with friends, and spend her money willy-nilly until she got a waitressing job. When she was thirteen a boy and his mom, who lived a block away, invited her over to watch a movie in the afternoon. When late evening arrived we called to find out when she would be home. She asked if she could stay for one more movie and his mom said it was okay. I asked her to put his mom on the phone. She of course was not there so Renee' came home. The crisis was averted and she did not try anything similar during high school. She was more worried about disappointing us than most children.

As she was nearing the end of high school Renee' started to rebel to the community college plan we had and wanted to go to a United Methodist four year college, in southern Kansas, where she had attended a Kiwanis Circle K Leadership Camp. For a couple of months Renee' continued to discuss the college, to speak with their admissions department, and to try to devise a way to convince me to let her attend. This became a growing source of contention and it also did not make economic sense. She kept stating the school would help her find financing for all but ten-thousand dollars a semester. This was all fine and good but the community college, on a cash basis, was less than three. Finally, considering the scholarships she received, Renee' would make a few dollars at the local school. My wife, in the end, sat her down, told her to quit acting like a spoiled brat, and to listen to her father. She did and is now paying the dividends of humility and submission. The resume' she was able to build while there was impressive and can be seen in the chapter on Resume's.

Chapter 6 - Study Abroad (Send Them Away)

When Renee' was a Junior in high school she came home from school one day very excited about a presentation given by Education First Tours (EF Tours). They are a domestic company that specializes in putting together educational trips for high schoolers to other countries.

At the time we lived in podunk America in Kansas. We decided Renee' needed to know there was a much bigger

world than Ohio, Colorado, and Kansas so we sent her to
Spain. She came back completely changed and definitely
was bitten by the travel bug.

The end of May 2014 she went on another trip, but this time
I went along with her. I took her to Sydney, Australia for her
high school graduation present, and we also attended the
International Rotary Club convention. Again, she was able
to see yet another part of the world and was exposed to
philanthropy on a large scale. One of the keynote speakers
was a parapalegic young man who was also on the United
Kingdom ParaOlympic Team. Because, at some point he
needed an Occupational Therapist, she saw other avenues
her new field could take her.

During her freshman year in college, at the local junior
college, the teacher who was instrumental in her visit to
Spain asked her to be a sponsor on their upcoming trip to
Italy, the Vatican City, and Paris, France. She of course
accepted and she rounded out a lot of international travel.
It was at this time we began to study the importance of, and
see the benefit of, being able to study abroad (expound).
Because our original plan was to have Renee' graduate with
her sociology degree from the University of Kansas we
decided to start by exploring their program to study
overseas. We sent many emails back and forth and the gist
was she would need to enroll with them then apply for their
study abroad program. They may have been affiliated with
other programmes in the United Kingdom, but I seem to
recall they may only have had a joint programme with the
University of Essex.

Part of our investigation turned up that Essex was ranked
22nd worldwide in sociological studies, the University of
Manchester was 20th, the University of Edinburgh was 14th,
but Oxford University was consistently ranked first or

second in the world. Because she was already enrolled with, and taking courses at, Wichita State University we also met with a counselor there to discuss their programme in the United Kingdom. Their studies are shared with the University of Chester and they happen to hold a ranking in sociology worldwide out of the top 100. When we met with the counselor we were told they had never seen a college path like the one we had devised because of the complexity and paths.

As a family we did much praying and soul-searching about what we should do and in the end we decided to go it alone. Financial aid seemed pretty easy to get if you went through a domestic overseas programme, but I researched it and found Renee' could still qualify through FAFSA if we simply did it ourselves. Around 40% of applications are accepted at Edinburgh, so it was not a "gimme", but we felt pretty good about her chances there.

There is an application process in the United Kingdom through UCAS at   https://www.ucas.com . The way it usually works is a student applies to Oxford or Cambridge. You are unable to apply to both universities in one year so you must choose one. If you are not accepted to the school you chose then you may apply to four more schools within the United Kingdom. We sat down with our daughter and discussed which university would be most advantageous. Again, Oxford was ranked first in the world for sociology, according to U.S. News & World Report, and Renee' had a friend from the Circle K Leadership Academy who attended for a year, and she wanted to apply to the best, so they won the bid. The first step in application to Oxford is a four hour long test that is similar to the ACT. It is held in a few cities across the United States so you must find dates and locations at http://www.ox.ac.uk/admissions/undergraduate/applying-to-oxford/guide/admissions-tests , and then plan accordingly. I flew Renee', and her mother for moral support, to the University of Florida at Jacksonville. I flew them in on a Friday night, and explained in another chapter everything they endured for the Saturday test.

After the test was complete we checked the application status continually. Eventually we received the rejection letter so we started the next application process. Because we had already researched college rankings in her chosen field we picked three top universities in the United Kingdom in sociological studies. The University of Manchester almost immediately rejected her application, which was okay as we were not completely sold on them either. She was almost as promptly accepted to the University of Essex which was the same one the University of Kansas was affiliated with. However, the school we really wanted at this point, the University of Edinburgh, was still a hold out and would be for a long time. I did a lot of study about this school, and also found it was known as the university for Oxbridge rejects or for those who were almost accepted at Oxford and Cambridge. The waiting dragged on and on. I even purchased the Scottish ale, Belhaven, and Drumguidich, the twenty year old single-malt scotch, to drink in solidarity with her hopefully new school. Sure enough, eventually Renee' received the email and subsequent postcard stating "Congratulations! You've been offered a place @ The University of Edinburgh School of Social & Political Science." That was a good day.

When we got the news we decided, as a family, we would take her to school. It would be an international family trip! My wife likened it to more of a mission than a trip or vacation. My poor family; I had everything pretty much planned from the minute we left Kansas to the day we returned. Okay, this may be an exaggeration, but I had a lot planned and tickets and Airbnb purchased.

STUDY ABROAD EXPANDED

In today's cultural, business, and educational climate studying, traveling, and philanthropy abroad are processes essential for current and prospective college students. Our world has become more close knit through airline travel, the internet, and up to videoconferencing. However, differing cultures and norms cannot be fully experienced and appreciated simply through a device. It must be lived in person.

Renee', as she studied in Scotland, was not simply away at school but was an ocean away! I placed the entirety of what we received from the Department of Education in her Royal Bank of Scotland account. We then made her produce her own budget and spend accordingly. She did well and actually had a small amount left at the end of the school year. We followed the same pattern when she attended her senior year at the University of Kansas, and now at Boston University Sargent College it is all her as the funds were disbursed directly to her.

Scottish culture was something she fully embraced and experienced as much as she could take in. She had pictures on her wall of the friends she had made through high school and two years of college. Renee' was distressed and mentioned in the United Kingdom people would typically make one or two friends and hang out with them at the pub. This was somewhat of a generalization. She loved to meet lots of people and make new friends and she was distressed by how difficult she found this to be in Edinburgh. I will say as she began to focus on changing the local culture she touched and could influence, she then made friends of students from Glasgow, Wales, Finland, China, Japan, Kosovo, Africa, Georgia, and Massachusett's. One of these friends, from the groups who were content to befriend one or two, mentioned the pictures on Renee's wall. She said, "you have a lot of friends. None of these pictures are of the same person."

She had experienced public transportation in Barcelona, Madrid, Rome, and Paris but Scotland was the first time she had to use it on a daily basis to commute to and from school. This took trip planning daily and some walking which made her healthier.

Another workout type activity she found were local caidh's. This is a Scottich dance which goes almost non-stop for hours. These were great social events for the students and extremely good exercise.

For the holidays she signed up for a woman's vocal choir that was planning to sell tickets to donate to charity. She made even more new friends from this group, had great fun, and they sounded very professional, well trained, and vocally gifted.

On New Year's Eve she and some friends attended the FESTIVAL and were in the hills outside of the city when the clock struck midnight. She told us how eerily beautiful it sounded when the entire city began to sing Auld Lang Syne in unison as it echoed from the mountains.

At the end, sending Renee' to study abroad did several things for her future. She was immersed in the fact the world is bigger than simply where we lived. Renee' fell in love with other cultures. She is exploring the possibility of finishing her Doctoral Capstone in the United Kingdom. She itches to travel and experience as much of the world as she possibly can. Her network is worldwide. To top it all off she is still wide-eyed with wonder and continues to dream big dreams.

EXPANDED

During her time in Edinburgh many good things happened. First, and foremost, she grew up and became an independent young woman. Mommy and Daddy were not in the next room, or next state, to run to in order to kiss her boo boo's goodbye. With today's technology, and especially WhatsApp, she could call, but problems were ultimately her own to figure out. Renee' learned how to budget and spend wisely.

As a family we learned the Scot's grade uni much differently than we do in the states. In the United Kingdom they expect the smart ones to carry "C's". Those making a "B" grade are borderline brilliant. "A's" are reserved for gifted students who are ready to be published authors based upon their field and research. There were many tears at this point as these were the lowest rash of grades Renee' ever had to this point. I am at least proud to say they ended up being "B's". I could live with them though she almost could not.

Another piece she learned, which still serves her today, was about public transportation in a large city. She was introduced to the concept though her EF Tours to Barcelona, Rome, and Paris. When she and I visited Sydney, Australia, I listened to her travel instructions while we were there and she never got us lost. Her skills were displayed prominently when we took Renee' to Edinburgh via Paris and London. She was familiar with the Paris system through EF Tours, London was simply common sense, but Edinburgh took all three of us to figure out. What a weird public transit system. When we took her to Boston she guided us in conjunction with google maps and travel was a breeze.

The pictures in Appendix A were when we dropped her off in Edinburgh and my wife and I were waiting for the train to London. There were tears from both of us. The other picture was when we picked her up at the Kansas City airport. This was the first time we had seen her in nine months and it was joyous!

One thing I remember Renee' mentioning was that the lectures and schoolwork were from professor's who were not simply teaching them from a book, but they were bringing information which was being utilized and learned in the "field". This was an exciting part of her learning experience.

Chapter 7 - Keep Your Eye On Classes and the Grades

When I say, "Keep Your Eye On Classes and the Grades", this is where my OCD kicked in. The grades are rather self explanatory, and I will get to those. What I mean by "Eye On Classes" I mean to make sure every class is taken which needs to be. There are a multitude of pre-requisites as well as certain classes that must be taken to graduate with a certain major.

I went back to college at the ripe old age of thirty-six, and pursued a Bachelor's Degree in Marketing. As I was reaching the point of graduating I decided to add a Master's Degree in Accounting & Finance. A year or so after graduation with my Master's I decided to pursue becoming a CPA. If I were litigation "happy" I would have sued the university that "sold" me my degree. They only missed having me take four or five classes necessary to become a CPA. Because of this I vowed not to miss anything Renee' needed to take, and I would take the responsibility upon myself.

For this part of the endeavor I created several spreadsheets to keep an eye, not only on her high school studies, but definitely her college ones. As mentioned elsewhere in this book I also "strong armed" her principal into letting her take algebra in eighth grade.

The first thing I did for the spreadsheet preparation was find the top three programs in her desired field, and I went to the Master's and Doctoral level. I entered into the spreadsheet all classes from all three schools required to graduate with a degree as an Occupational Therapist. I then broke all of those classes down into what pre-requisites were required in order to sign up for those classes, and entered those into the spreadsheet. I kept scouring backwards and broke all prerequisite course into their simplest form until there were no more prerequisite requirements.

At this point I moved to the bachelor level and entered into the spreadsheet all classes in sociology, our chosen field, from three desired universities. All prerequisites from those classes were also broken down to their simplest form until the first classes had no requisite requirements. This is when the OCD fun began!

Beginning with her college classes in high school, including her intro to Anatomy and Physiology, I started putting "X" in the cell next to the listed class in the spreadsheet. As each enrollment period rolled around for uni we would consult the spreadsheet, pick the next prerequisites on the list, add some electives, and make sure a good chunk was taken out of the spreadsheet bite. When we reached the point of applying for her post graduate studies she was qualified to attend all programs because she had taken every possible prerequisite for them. The spreadsheets I used can be found at:
https://drive.google.com/drive/folders/1TYW5MSGIeij0y8bp0xR7Uh5qUShG8zL7?usp=sharing

Now, back to grades. Renee' was blessed with a good portion of intelligence whereas not all students are. However, what we found is a tutor can cure many ills. Renee' tutored many other students throughout high school and college who would have otherwise failed their classes. Her grades were predominantly A's with smatterings of a B here and there. It was not until the second semester of her doctoral program she made her first C. There were tears. I would suggest, if your student will be making B's and below, you find a tutor for each subject they are struggling in. High school grades were much more important to Renee's success than test scores, but you will need to make sure they are A's and maybe some B's.

Chapter 8 - Don't Sweat the Tests - much (ACT/SAT/GRE) Testing. Oh the bane of Renee's college application existence. I want to reiterate my daughter is extremely intelligent. However, that brilliance did not transfer well to the standardized testing process. In high school she seemed to test well in each of her classes. This all changed when she had to take the ACT. She is every bit as smart as I am, and I believe more so. The difference is I love tests and Renee' had test anxiety. I took the ACT one time, did not take it very seriously, and scored a 32. I made my poor daughter take it three times. The first time she scored a 25. The second time she took it she was very ill, and only eked out a 26. The third time she was not ill, but still only managed a repeat 26. At this point we decided a 26 was about as good as it was going to get.

The junior college she planned to attend had two presidential level scholarships. Her 26 did not qualify her for the academic one even though her high school GPA was a high A. However, with a commitment to volunteer hours, as alluded to in the chapter on Community Service, she did qualify for the Presidential Leadership Scholarship. This was the only time her ACT score was used or needed for college acceptance.

Renee's ACT "is what it is" and we ran with the score she gave us. We sought a different outcome on the GRE, or Master's level test. We used some of the resources from Appendix A, and then she buckled down and did the most intense study of her life. This was during the first semester of her fourth "brick and mortar" undergraduate degree and fifth actual college year. She was taking her largest, per credit hour, and most difficult semester in the Fall, but she made the schedule work. We booked the test date then broke down the number of weeks and days until test time. Then we divided all different study materials into those number of days. I found, through a search of Princeton University, students learn subjects from three mediums. They learn aurally or through spoken lectures. Students learn visually or through video, powerpoints, reading, or other ways as seen through their eyes. Those learning also retain information kinesthetically or by "doing". This is also known as "hands on". During Renee's study for the GRE we tried to incorporate all three ways of learning, or studying daily. These were also how she was taught at age 4 through our Bowling Green, Ohio Montessori pre-school. Renee' remained faithful and studied a little each day with all three variations of learning. Unlike the ACT she only took the GRE test once. Her final results were: she killed it!

If your student tests well then there is not much I can add here. However, if your's is like mine, and testing is a curse, there are things you can do to improve or bypass the outcome. The first step, of course, is to study, study, study. There are whole other books and podcasts on this subject so

I will not tell you how they should study. I will simply provide resources in Appendix A.

When she applied to "uni" in the United Kingdom a different test score, and system, was used. In the chapter about studying abroad we cover the process and thoughts behind it in more detail. Renee's first three years of college were effectively accomplished in two as she took "brick and mortar" classes from Wichita State University while attending junior college. When we decided she should study abroad we found the ACT's would not be used as we decided to "go it alone" and not send her under a domestic university's umbrella. She takes after me and dreams just as big if not bigger. As we narrowed down the foriegn college fields, and decided we were going to start with Oxford, we also found they had their own proprietary test.

At http://www.ox.ac.uk/admissions/undergraduate/applying-to-oxford/guide/admissions-tests you can find test locations and dates for the Oxford test. The most convenient, and the test that most worked with our schedule, was all the way down in Florida. In all of my wisdom I decided to fly her to Florida on Friday, she would stay in an inexpensive (cheap) motel, test on Saturday morning, then fly back the afternoon of the test. My wife went with her for moral support and, to this day, they will not let me forget putting them up in a fleabag motel. The toilet was dirty, the room had mold (hey, it was Florida), and they slept in their clothes on top of the bed covers because they were so dirty. Maybe this played into Renee's lack of success, or her non-acceptance to Oxford. However, Essex and Edinburgh both decided her test scores were good enough for their schools.

We knew once Renee' was accepted into a program she would do well, and they would pat themselves on the back for letting her in. The problem was going to be getting accepted based on low test scores. The best way, we decided, was to create a path not solely contingent upon the score on a test. We were often told no-one had ever seen a college path, or career, like Renee's.

Chapter 9 - Application Process - Domestic, International, Graduate

The application process for Domestic colleges and universities can be found generally on their website. That is how Renee' applied to her junior college, the state university where she took conjoining classes, and then the final year of her bachelor's degree at the University of Kansas. When she applied in the United Kingdom, as referenced elsewhere within this book, she had to first apply to either Oxford or Cambridge, you cannot apply to both at the same time, and then when rejected by one or the other you may apply to four other universities within the United Kingdom without paying more money.

One thing to keep in mind, I have mentioned in other places, is to find universities well ranked internationally within your child's chosen field of study. Again, a great resource will be   https://www.usnews.com/best-colleges It holds a plethora of useful information. (I simply wanted to use plethora in a sentence.)

Chapter 10 - Interviewing Successfully and Follow Up To Interview

The call, email, or letter came and the school would like to interview your child. Congratulations! Now, just like they did before the test time it is time to study.

As an interview is to finding a job, and a face-to-face is to closing the sale, so the school interview is as well and is basically the same as a job interview.

In Renee's interview letter it stated she could work in a school visit while she was there, she could interview in person, or they could set up a video call if she could not travel to Boston.

I wanted the interviewers to see her passion for the field she wanted to go into and I did not believe that a video call could adequately convey her burning desire for the field. For this reason we begged and borrowed to put her on a plane to the east coast. My wife only calls me "Mr. Rage" when "I done good", and after her acceptance letter came my wife told me, "Mr. Rage", it was brilliant sending her to Boston." Am I blushing?

As it came time for her to prepare thoroughly for the interview we visited several websites to look at possible interview questions and avenues. You will never know what will be asked or discussed so you must cover a wide gamut in order for your student to adequately represent themselves.

It is similar to playing a musical instrument. Once you have the exercises, chords, and differing melodies ingrained in your muscle memory it becomes simple to ad lib and make these things part of a larger song.

The interviewers asked Renee' what she likes to do for fun. Baking is a skill that can be taught through Occupational Therapy and as an ADL (activity of daily living) as it helps give autonomy back to patients. Our daughter had spent the last two years teaching students from the United States, the United Kingdom, Eastern Europe, and Asia how to bake. Her favorite pastime, to go with this activity she told them, was "kitchen karaoke". This was around the time "Carpool

Karaoke" was being made internationally popular by James Corden.

Before she left for the interview, I told her if they were looking for a diverse candidate then she probably was not it. It was at this point Renee' developed another story. During the spring of her year at the University of Kansas she attended a diversity conference sponsored by the Christian Union. Friday evening a group of students went to see the new movie, "Black Panther". The group was made up of predominately students of African racial origin. Renee' chose to go with them because they were her friends, and because she wanted to feel what it was like being a minority in a group. When she told this to the interviewers, one of them put down her pen, looked her in the eye, and told her how inspiring it was. When Renee' told me the story I told her this was the moment she was accepted to the program.

Well, the interview is out of the way and I hope it was in person. Now comes the most important step in the process. This is the follow up. Rather than give pointers I will simply give the story of what we had Renee' do.

Because we flew her to Boston it would be a day or so before she was home and could begin to do follow up. For this reason I had her prepare a hand written "thank you" note for the interviewers. Before she left campus, the plan was for her to personalize the note with the interviewers names, to subtly mention a key part of the interview they would remember, and then give this note to the student assistant. What Renee' added was the phrase, "looking forward to karaoke with you in the future" and she did give it to the assistant.

Another way we could have pulled this off would be to have the note ready, have your student call home with names and the interview tie-in, have you write the note, then mail it from your hometown so the stamp would be from your post office. This would get it there a little faster than waiting for your child to fly home, and would give it the local post office "feel" which would be a good thing also.

That is all of the follow up I would suggest as you do not want to seem pushy or needy at this point.

Chapter 11 - Pray and Then Celebrate

As we waited to hear from the United Kingdom on her study abroad program we thought we were developing patience. That was wrong. Our patience was developed during the wait for the Master's/Doctoral Program. It was an excruciating wait for notification from the first Occupational Therapy school.

The University of Kansas notified us first that she had not been accepted. So much for graduating from there with her Bachelor's Degree. They were also the only program that added application fees for some essay. I was not impressed. It did not matter much in the scheme of things. They were only ranked 9th in the United States.

Second on the notification list was the University of Spoi… I mean Southern California. They were ranked number three on the list, and they also turned Renee' down. At this point we only had two schools left in play. This is when we started to get nervous. That is why I would suggest maybe applying to six to eight schools.

The University of Washington Saint Louis, who was tied for first in the country, sent her an email next stating that she had not been accepted on the first wave, but they would put her name on the waitlist. She sent them a follow up email to make sure they knew she was still interested.

Great, now we were down to one. Boston University - Sargent College was the lone hold out. They were tied for first in the nation, and were the only Doctoral program on the list so I figured if they said "no" then we could start applying to online schools or something. We had been praying through this whole process, we knew YHVH would make things turn out the way He wanted them to, but depression was on the horizon.

I remember driving my tow truck in Colorado, on Airport Road in Rifle, heading west past Walmart, when I got a call from Renee'. She was crying. Whenever she cries her mother makes her call me so I can talk her out of the tree. I was sure Boston had finally said "no".

"Dad", she said, "Boston sent me an email today. They want me in their program!"

Appendix A

School Rankings

https://www.usnews.com/info/blogs/press-room/articles/2019-10-22/us-news-announces-2020-best-global-universities-rankings

https://www.usnews.com/education/best-global-universities/search?region=&subject=social-sciences-public-health&name=

https://www.usnews.com/education/best-high-schools/rankings-overview

Job Rankings

https://www.usnews.com/info/blogs/press-room/articles/2020-01-07/us-news-reveals-the-2020-best-jobs

Application Portal - United Kingdom

https://www.ucas.com/

Interview Preparation Tips

https://bigfuture.collegeboard.org/get-in/interviews/college-interviews-practice-questions-and-strategies

https://www.princetonreview.com/college-advice/college-interview-tips

https://www.gradschools.com/get-informed/applying-graduate-school/graduate-school-interview/graduate-school-interview-questions

http://www.wiu.edu/student_services/career_development_center/decision/pdf/GraduateSchoolInterviewingTips.pdf

Spreadsheets for Prerequisites

This is the link to a viewable Google doc that shows my psychosis:

https://drive.google.com/file/d/0B3ck2MES2gPOSVgxZklIRFN4RjQ/view?usp=sharing

Name	Number	Hours	
College Algebra	MA106	3.0	
College Trigonometry	MA107	3.0	
English Composition I	EN101	3.0	
English Composition II	EN102	3.0	
General Biology	BI101	4.0	
Intro To Leadership	ED118	3.0	
General Psychology	PS100	3.0	
Elem Spanish I	SP101	5.0	
Soc Dance-Beg	PE151	1.0	
Human Growth & Development	PS102	3.0	
Public Speaking	SH101	3.0	
Elem Spanish II	SP102	5.0	
Art Appreciation	AR101	3.0	
Human A&P/Lab - Lecture	BI103	6.0	
World History To 1600	HI103	3.0	
Intro to Literature	EN201	3.0	
Ethics	PL104	3.0	
Abnormal Psychology	PS202	3.0	
New Testament Literature	RE101	3.0	
Student Government I	SG111	1.0	
Student Government II	SG112	1.0	
Student Government III	SG113	1.0	
Student Government IV	SG114	1.0	
Cultural Anthropology	ANTH102	3.0	3
Medical Terminology	HP203	3.0	3
Intro To Sociology	SOC111	3.0	3
Intro To Global Health Issues	HMCD327	3.0	3
Young Women's Health	SOC337	3.0	3
Intro US Health Service Systems	HMCD310	3.0	3
Sociology of Aging	SOC513	3.0	3
The Social Consequences of Disability	SOC537	3.0	3

Name	Number	Hours	
Medical Sociology	SOC538	3.0	3
		94.0	27

Course Name	Course #	Hours Taken	Hours Needed	
Art Appreciation	AR101		3	3 Associate of Arts
Drawing I	AR110			3 HCC
Human A&P	BI103	6	6	
Success Seminar/College Orie	ED105	no	1	
English Comp II	EN102	3	3	
World History to 1600	HI103	3	3	
World History since 1600	HI104		3	
Medical Terminology	HR105	3	3	
College Algebre	MA106	3	3	
Elements of Statistics	MA108	Spring	3	
Personal and Community Hea	PE105		3	
Ethics	PL104	Spring	3	
General Psychology	PS100	3	3	
Abnormal Psychology	PS202	Spring	3	
Public Speaking	SH101	3	3	
Fundamentals of Sociology	SO100	SO111	3	
Biology Options	BI101	4	4	
Chemistry Options			5	
English Comp I			3	
Religion Options		Spring	3	
not more than 60 in SO		Total Hours	64	
Introduction To Sociology	SO111	3	3 Bachelors - Sociology	
Introduction To Social Researc	SO312		3 WSU	
Sociological Statistics	SO501		3	
Measurement and Analysis	SO512		3	
Sociological Theory	SO545		3	
		Total Hours		
Sociology of Aging	SO513	3		
College Trigonometry		3		
English Comp I	EN101	3		
Cultural Anthropology	ANTH102	3		
Intro To Global Health Issues	HMCD327	3		
Young Womens Health	SOC337	3		
Social Dance	PE151	1		
Human Growth & Developmer	PS102	3		
Student Govt I	SG111	1		
Student Govt II	SG112	1		
Student Govt III	SG113	1		
Student Govt IV	SG114	Spring		
Elementary Spanish I	SP101	5		
Elementary Spanish II	SP102	5		
Intro To Leadership	ED118	3		

I

Class Name	Class Number	Hours	Finished?	
Elements of Sociology	SOC 104		SOC 111	KU
	Math 101		Done	
any	SOC			
Intro to Social Research	SOC 310			
any 3 or over	SOC 3		SOC 337	
any 3 or over	SOC 3		SOC 513	
Elementary Statistics and l	SOC 510			
any 3 or over	SOC 3			
any 3 or over	SOC 3			
Sociological Theory	SOC 500			
any 3 or over	SOC 3		SOC 538	
any 3 or over	SOC 3		SOC 537	
Intro to Sociology	SOC 111		Done	WSU
Intro to Social Research	SOC 312			
Sociological Statistics	SOC 501			
Measurement and Analysi	SOC 512			
Sociological Theory	SOC 545			124 hours

Renee' leaving us, at the Edinburgh Waverley railway station, to begin her year at the University of Edinburgh.

Renee' coming off of the plane, at the Kansas City International Airport, after her year at uni.

Peaks - by Alexis M. Rage

At age 35 I woke up one day and found myself a very unhealthy 250 pounds, and a far cry from where I was when I married at 25. In high school, I was a runner. My favorite book was "A Father, a Son, and a Three-Mile Run" by Keith J. Leenhouts, about a father's love and help for his son who was developing non-typically. During the fall, my life was 3.1-mile cross-country meets in fields and on golf-courses. When spring hit, I was pumping out one- and two-milers around the track. In a moment of brilliance during a cross-country meet in El Dorado, Kansas, I was the lead runner at the midpoint of the race. Unfortunately, I faded quickly and finished the race near mid-pack on rubbery legs. My love for running did not lead to a passion for training hard. Years later, I struggled to run a half-mile without being winded and exhausted. Deciding to run again to lose excess weight, and regain some health, was going to be hard work.

My grandfather had his first heart attack at age 50. He passed away in his seventies having suffered two more, as well as two debilitating strokes. To avoid contributing to this family "legacy," and to combat post traumatic stress disorder, my father began running when he returned from his tour in Vietnam. Now, at 77, he is the picture of health for his age, having never experienced heart problems or strokes. His example fostered my love of running. At age 35, I signed up for the November Kansas City Marathon in 2003, bought a book about training for my first marathon, and subscribed to Runner's World Magazine. I trained, lost 20 pounds, and finished the race in 5 hours, 0 minutes, and 41 seconds. After the race, I mentally checked a marathon off of my bucket list, and never needed to do that again...so I ran four more. Two in 2004, Disney in 2006, and the Oklahoma City Memorial in 2001. I even decided to train for an Ironman Triathlon.

In 2006 my family moved to my dream spot in the Vail Valley of Colorado. That June, I discovered the 10K Spring Runoff, with the Teva Mountain Games. This diabolical 10Kish race (7 miles rather than the typical 6.2) enjoys shooting its runners straight up the black diamond ski slopes 5 or 6 times before letting them meander their way down beautiful mountain trails just to shoot us straight back up the side of the mountain again. For some crazy reason, I fell in love with mountain running.

June 2007, a week after finishing my second year of the 10K Spring Runoff, I was working two jobs and training for my first Ironman. On a Sunday like many others, we went to church and ate lunch. I took a short nap, and then got on my Trek triathlon-configured road bicycle to ride the Glenwood Canyon trail for my bike training.

It is because of YHVH (the Tetragrammaton for God) that I am here today to write this. I still do not remember anything, but pieced this together based on hearsay. Just west of Gypsum, Colorado, where we lived at the time, there is a sharp "U" on the bike trail which goes around a gully and a tree. When I recreated the conditions, I realized I have a tendency to raise myself from my triathlon aerobars with my right hand first. This happens to be the side that operates the front brake. On that Sunday, I flipped my bike, landed on my head leaving my helmet broken, slid into the gully, and was found a while later by a couple walking their dog. Upon finding me, I was unresponsive, so they Life Flighted me to Grand Junction's St. Mary's Hospital. There I was diagnosed with a traumatic brain injury (TBI) of which good recoveries are not promised.

It took a week or so to start coming out of my brain fog, and I think I know what St. Mary's Hospital kind of looks like. However, as I was coming to know the facility, my wife moved me closer to home: Valley View Hospital in Glenwood Springs, Colorado. I spent a few weeks recovering there, followed by a long stint as both an inpatient and outpatient at Craig Hospital in Englewood, Colorado. They are known worldwide for their spinal cord injury and TBI recovery programs.

47

Over the course of the next year, we moved back to central Kansas to be near family. I held many jobs, but could not seem to stay with one for very long as I was on anti-depressant medication to ensure my brain was generatingserotonin, which is common after a TBI. My serotonin reuptake inhibitor kept me one degree above depressed and I never felt true joy. This time in my life was agonizing. Fortunately, during one of my job changes, I lost my health insurance and had to forgo my medications "cold-turkey."

I took up running again, began to experience the wild symptoms of "cold-turkey," and bawled like a baby every time I heard "Rooftops" by Jesus Culture. I found aerobic exercise helped produce brain-derived neurotrophic factor, or BDNF, which in turn helped with serotonin generation! In other words, running made me feel great. In May 2011, my father and I finished an epic Oklahoma City Memorial Marathon which boasted 20 degree wind chills, bouts of hail, and rain during the entire run. The next year, we finished the Vail Pass Half Marathon from Vail, Colorado to Vail Pass (Yes, this meant there were no stretches of downhill running!). It was after this run I realized I enjoyed ascending mountains, to which my friends say there may be some loose wires in my brain. Most of them have no idea how close to right they are.

I spent much of my 49th year driving between the western slope of Colorado (where I worked) and central Kansas. I commuted ten hours twice a month to see my wife at home. When I wasn't driving I was training for my first 14er (the summit of a fourteen-thousand-foot mountain). High-altitude pulmonary edema can happen at this elevation, and oxygen is reduced to less than 60% of what it is at sea level.

I decided I wanted to do my first 14er the day I turned 50. A complicated goal: the week of my 50th birthday, we as a family were taking my daughter to her entry-level doctorate of occupational therapy program, at Boston University Sargent College, via Niagara Falls in Canada. On my commute home, to Kansas, I stopped at a pizza parlor in Silverthorne, Colorado to carbo-load, and then drove up to the parking area for Grays Peak just off of I-70, east of the Eisenhower Tunnel.

I took a nap before beginning my trek up the side of the mountain, just west of the beautiful Continental Divide. I began at a lovely 3 am. The light of the full moon meant I could walk without my headlamp. The time I spent walking and conversing with YHVH was glorious.

Several years before this hike I read a devotional called "A Look at Life from a Deer Stand" by Steven Chapman. In the book, Steven goes to the mountains of Alaska for a moose hunt. He mentions that his guide, Petrich, makes intentional stops during the hunt to give Steven a chance to look at the beautiful scenery. Halfway through the hunt, Steven realizes that Petrich is actually slyly giving him a chance to catch his breath even though Steven had worked out often in preparation for the excursion. Stopping often to enjoy the view, and to refresh, became known as "The Petrich Method."

During my hike to the top of Grays Peak I was determined to quit no fewer than 50 times. I also had a nagging thought in the back of my mind that, if I quit, I would never come back to try it again. Throughout the entire trek "The Petrich Method" kept coming to mind. My legs would move 100 steps and I would stop for a minute. Then I would repeat the process. Around 9 o'clock in the morning, six hours later, it finally paid off. I reached the summit of my first 14er and claimed victory over my brain injury!

Since that time, I have found my dream job, or calling, in our local prison as a correction's counselor. Many offenders on my caseload have TBI's of their own, and I can empathize somewhat when their understanding of life may be skewed. I can look back to see YHVH's hand in my journey here and look forward with confidence to whatever race comes next. Also, I have completed two more 14er's, a 13er, and have qualified for the Pikes Peak Ascent (another 14er) for August of 2022.

Grays Peak
14,270'
08/29/2018

Mt. Evans
14,265'
08/29/2019

Mt. Spalding
13,842'
08/29/2019

Mount Bierstadt
14,065'
08/29/2020